BLESS MY GROWING

for parents, teachers,
and others who learn

GERHARD E. FROST

Photographs by Doug Messmer

AUGSBURG PUBLISHING HOUSE
MINNEAPOLIS, MINNESOTA

BLESS MY GROWING

Copyright © 1974 Augsburg Publishing House

Library of Congress Catalog Card No. 74-77680

International Standard Book No. 0-8066-1431-5

Manufactured in the United States of America

To my sister Esther,
a life-long teacher
who lived with learners
and heard their cries

CONTENTS

KNOW SOMETHING

"Know something,"
The old man tersely said.
It was his counsel to
one who would teach.

If I am a teacher,
(and all of us are),
I will prove my love by knowing.
I will never cease to inquire,
for love always wants to know.

Some of the greatest teachers haven't spoken
much about love,
but they've pressed hard for knowledge,
and whatever they've known they've shared.
They haven't withheld themselves.

Youth is not served
by nervous concern,
but by steady availability
and openness of heart and mind.
Teaching is shared humanity
in relation to something known
or needing to be known.
The old man was right.

I STILLED A SONG

The seventh of May:
I stilled a song today.

A meadow lark flew up from the grass
as I sped by;
I had no time to avoid the crash.
I saw the broken body fall
as I stole a glance at the rearview mirror.

I can't tell where the bird was going
when I killed it:
I only know that it was on its way
from song to song,
for that's the way a meadow lark flies
in spring.

It will never sing again.

I think of myself, a teacher and parent, and wonder
how often have I killed an imagination
or darkened a dream?
How often have I stilled a song?

It is no small thing
to kill a song.

THE DEMON SELF-DOUBT

He'd had a great year
in kindergarten,
but now the going was hard
in first grade.
After reflection and brooding,
he came to his mother
with a sad self-assessment
and solemn conclusion:
"I don't think I'm really first grade;
I'm more kindergarten type."

For another, it had been a significant career,
seventy years of hard
and responsible work.
But now he sat alone,
downcast and discouraged.
As I approached him with a greeting he said:
"I'm no good; I can't work at anything any more."

Two persons,
each with a given dignity
and "justified by faith,"
both deep in self-evaluation
and suffering
at the hands of the demon, Self-doubt,
both at a crossroad
and needing wise and compassionate friends.

Voices are needed,
my voice and yours,
voices of self-appointed guardians
of the fragile egos
of the very young and very old,
and everyone between,
voices to proclaim
that God has loved us
into dignity and worth forever.

ATTICS

There's something about attics
that can mesmerize and paralyze.
They're good for "tripping,"
and forgetting this present world.
It's best not to risk a visit to the attic
unless one is prepared to let "twenty minutes"
become half a day.

The "I remember room,"
it brings lumps to the throat
or chuckles of recollection.
With half a century for forgetting
I smell our attic yet,
and see it, too.
Seed-corn drying by the chimney,
National Geographics piled against the wall,
sentimental throw-aways that just wouldn't be thrown,
and things outgrown or out of date.

One needs to visit the attic of the heart,
the musty, back spaces of the mind,
to bring to remembrance the days
when one clung to too small a God
and confessed an inadequate creed,
too cramped for the human situation.

It is well that we visit our attics,
but, as mother used to say,
"Don't drag things down."

There's beauty and deep meaning in the attic,
but it mustn't be the living room.
It's not for changing,
just remembering,
And to live is always to change.

AN EARLY CRY

Only two, and true to us all,
she loved a story.
Her name: Rachel, but when she said it,
it came out as "Rechu."

On this particular evening
nothing was right;
bumps, bruises, frustrations and disappointments
had drawn her to me,
and she stood with her curly head
bent into my lap,
hiding two tear-stained cheeks.

It was then that I said,
"Shall granddaddy tell you a story
about two horses who could run fast?"
Without a moment's lift of the head,
"No 'tory horses!"
came the uncapitulating reply.
I tried again, "Shall I tell you a story
about a nice man who had two little puppies?"
Again, with no less spirit and emphasis,
"No 'tory nice man!"

Then, not anticipating her response
or realizing my wisdom at the moment, I said,
"Shall I tell you a story about Rachel?"
Now, for the first time, the little head moved
and two eyes looked up, " 'tory Rechu?"
The bait was just too good,
and the little mourner was caught
in the net of excitement and self-interest.

I've wondered since,
may it not be that we've told too many stories
about horses that can run fast,
and nice men with puppies,
and have often forgotten to put
the Rachels and Richards, the Tommies and Trudys,
in the middle of the situation?
The cry for relevance is an early cry.

A GREAT MOMENT

When I think of her
and her gift to me,
I bless her and hope
that her number will increase.

It was the very first day
at a summer retreat,
and we sat in a circle in an abandoned barn.
I was the designated leader
and hoped that they would respond
and soon participate.

Hesitantly I sent up my "trial balloon,"
reaching for them by reading
a chosen passage that meant much to me.
Half-way through the reading,
with no one expecting it,
she exclaimed, "Wow!"

It was what I needed,
an ice-breaker and heart-warmer.
I relaxed and they took part,
each beginning to tell a little
of his or her "story."
We had a good week together,
thanks to one who dared to say, "Wow!"

In this cold world
why is it so hard
to be supportive of another?
Why is it dangerous to offer
one's gift of enthusiasm and response?
Why don't we dare to be "wow"
to one another?

ALL OVER AGAIN

It was a quiet lane,
one of the many in that Wisconsin wood
at the spacious retreat ground
where we were staying,
my friend and I.

We walked and talked,
for our friendship
went back to school days,
and here we were,
past middle age.
The swift years had brought gifts,
as they always do,
of memorable joys
and chastening sorrows.

We had married at about the same time,
but after very few years
his wife had died.
We spoke of that, and I said,
"You've been places
where I haven't been;
you've learned things
that I can't really know."
"Yes," he said, "But one has to learn them
all over again!"

His words checked me then
and have disturbed me since.
Perhaps this is the significance of sorrow,
that it underscores and rehearses
great meanings, so that,
in the round of daily experiences,
we do not lose them.

VIOLENT HANDS

The Western range was alive today,
alive with newborn calves,
and tonight I think of them.

A little bull calf was born today.
He will dance and frolic for a while,
but rough hands will seize him
and castrate him, leaving him
without spirit or pride.
He will feed on the range in his docile way,
but not for long,
for they will herd him with many others
into the crowded feed lot,
where he will stand for hours
growing soft and fat.
One day the blow will fall,
the knife will flash, and he will die—
a consumer to be consumed.

Another little bull calf was born today.
No violent hand will be laid on him.
He will roam free.
His sharp hooves will paw the ground
and throw dirt upon his back.
He will bellow his pride into the wind
and fight for every right
as he challenges each trespasser in his domain.
Many years he will roam
before he dies, fulfilled.

Is it so with The System?
Do we lay violent hands on the child?
Do we assault his individuality
And herd him into affluent sterility,
preparing him only to be a consumer
and to be consumed?

THE LONELIEST OUTPOSTS

They would call it a dying town,
and some would say that it is a lonely place,
so I asked my two young friends,
"Do you sometimes feel lonely here?"
They looked at each other, hesitated a moment,
then mentioned some things that brought them fulfillment.
And then the young husband said,
"And then, of course, we have Gilbert."

Gilbert is an aged arthritic,
living next door,
living his unique life,
with his spirited and devoted wife.
As we sat talking, one of them suddenly said,
"There's Gilbert now!" And there he came,
on his way to work in his garden.
Slowly and painfully he worked his way
toward the garden, leaning heavily on his "walker."
Beside him walked his wife, carrying a chair.
When he was in the right spot, she placed the chair.
Then she brought a spade and a long-handled rake.

Gilbert laid the rake carefully across his lap,
then with tremendous effort, pushed with both his feet
until the spade was in the ground,
then slowly turned the spade-full of soil.
Placing his spade across his lap,
he painstakingly broke up the newly turned ground.
Patiently he repeated this process
until he would have to raise himself from the chair
while his wife moved it to another spot.

We watched him work for a while,
such a contrast from the easy efficiency
of modern mechanized methods,
but so expressive of human greatness.

If we look for them, we, too, have our Gilberts,
manning the loneliest outposts of courage and perseverance,
and showing us where the fiercest battles of faith
are fought and won.

WE LIVE ON GLIMPSES

We live on glimpses,
fleeting glimpses in the forest;
this is its beauty,
this its charm.

A bit of furry fluff
disappearing behind a log,
the flash of a many-colored wing
telling us that a bird is hiding in the bush.
Wild things always in flight,
leaving us wishing for more,
more time to examine and admire,
more to hold in the hand.

We live on glimpses and wish for time-exposures;
but perhaps this is best:
to see wild things in the open,
untamed and free,
not caged or constrained, but free to go away.
For beauties are enhanced when they are fleeting;
they leave us hungry still.

We live on glimpses of great truths,
wild truths, like the fact of God's saving love.
To teach is never to tame or domesticate;
it is to acquaint each other
with truth on the wing,
unpredictable, unmanageable,
truth that seeks and seizes,
and will not be captured or contained.

BLESS MY GROWING

Lord, I've been wondering:
Why do I say *I*?
Why must I ask why?
Why is joy so close to pain?
Why do I feel transparent in the presence of a child?
Why am I often lonely in a crowd?
Why are people so sober before a clock? And a ten dollar bill?
Why am I so loud when I'm wrong? Or so fierce when I'm afraid?
Why is the human face most beautiful when it is looking up?
Why, in moments of crisis, do people either curse or pray?
Why does prosperity drive us apart?
And adversity bring us together?
Why is it painful to celebrate alone?
Why does my ability to ask questions
exceed my capacity to receive answers?
Why am I a mystery even to myself?
Lord, give me the right questions, and bless my growing.

WE WALK ON WATER

"But I never feel prepared!"
It was at a winter retreat
that a student said it,
and he spoke with the anguish of deep sincerity.
I was pleased when a counselor replied,
"But we walk on water all the time."

It is well to be prepared,
but we dare not forget that we are never fully prepared
for the tasks that are most worth doing.
The tasks that are worthy of us, as persons,
are often beyond us.
This is true of the challenge
of teaching.

Perhaps there is no effort
which is as total,
or which makes one so vulnerable
as teaching.
He who attempts it reaches beyond himself
and senses that his best is not good enough.
Humbling as it is, this work must not
discourage us.

As Christians, we who teach
truly walk on water all the time.
It is frightening until one remembers—
remembers and listens—
for across the broad waters comes the Voice, saying,
"Fear not, it is I."

LET IT LIVE

Never kill a question;
it is a fragile thing.
A good question deserves to live.
One doesn't so much answer it as converse with it,
or, better yet, one lives with it.
Great questions are the permanent
and blessed guests of the mind.
But the greatest questions of all
are those which build bridges to the heart,
addressing the whole person.

No answer should be designed to kill the question.
When one is too dogmatic, or too sure,
one shows disrespect for truth
and the question which points toward it.
Beyond my answer there is always more,
more light waiting to break in,
and waves of inexhaustible meaning
ready to break against wisdom's widening shore.
Wherever there is a question, let it live!

IT'S BEEN A LONG DAY

It's been a long day,
a very long day,
for I've been breaking in a pair of shoes.
My feet hurt.
As a friend used to say,
"My dogs are barking!"

But now I think of myself,
called to teach,
and I reflect on those shoes.
The experts gave me the right size;
it isn't their fault.
They've done what they could;
now it's up to me.
My foot must shape my shoe.

The trouble with new shoes
is that they don't feel;
they haven't learned to sympathize;
they just don't understand.

The specialist can generalize—
offer materials, conduct polls,
make suggestions for teaching—
but he can't know me
or my class, or this parish
with its many personalities and needs,
its expectations and frustrations.
It's up to me.

I'm it.
Lord, help me to trust you
and my own intuitions,
to really believe
that you're with me.

THE MOVEMENT OF GRACE

Like ocean waves,
beating against wet rocks
and washing miles of shore,
so the "blesseds" bear in upon me.
In them God's mercy comes,
and always there's more!
This is the movement of grace,
always toward me.
The inheritance seeks the heir.

It is a loving plan,
God's plan for me,
his purpose to pursue.
I run after the good,
but the best runs after me.
The Hound of Heaven is on my trail.
(I hear the "blesseds,"
and in them the baying of the Hound.)

"The only thing there's enough of,"
and it seeks me,
not *it*, but *he;*
he seeks me.
This is the grain of my existence,
and it is a gracious plan.
Even so, come, Lord Jesus.

RESPECT THE MOMENT

Like a person,
a question has to be warm
or it is dead.

One has to feel one's question.

Not, "We're coming to that,"
or, "We've had that."
In learning together
we've never had it;
we're always in it.

Teacher,
respect the moment.
It will never come again.

THE LIVED LIFE

I remember a little pair of shoes.
For months they stood side by side
on the closet floor,
begging for feet.

We had an active four-year-old
who ran and danced through the days
with always new plans for the morrow.
But one day she lay still
in a distant hospital
while the weeks went by.
It was polio.

We had shopped for shoes
and she loved hers especially
because they were her first that tied.
I remember praying,
as we put them aside,
that they would be worn again.

That experience taught me
that it is high privilege
to support life.
Never since have I complained
about the price of children's shoes.
Life is meant to beget and sustain more life.
To grow tired is not tragedy
if one is living by loving,
dying by giving.

The call to discipleship
is to "come and die,"
usually not in one burst of effort
or in a single pool of blood,
but in the steady self-draining
of life-strength and energy.

There's no room for self-pity
in the lived life.
Only the unlived quality
of our existence
should ever make us sad.

ONE MORE

Teacher,
when you've worked hard
and nothing happens,
when you've prepared well
but nothing comes off,
when every thought
crashes on the runway
and the whole lesson trails on the ground—
then, don't forget,
yes, don't forget
to count One more than
you can see!

THAT LOUDEST SOUND

There are burdens of meaning
which shatter speech,
splitting language at the seams
and leaving the loudest sound of all:
wonder-filled silence.
Such are the *O God* moments,
times when prayer trails off beyond sound,
when griefs and joys are too deep
for articulation.

God reads us,
unerringly hears our thoughts
and understands language
that leaves all words behind.

To be a person is to hold a secret,
and to have feelings too deep for sharing,
the secret at the center of one's being,
that secret which calls for sharing
only with him who is meant to possess us.

Respect for person means
to leave much to silence
because one leaves all to God.

THE EGO MUST EAT

I had promised to bring her home
from kindergarten that day.

As we were leaving,
a few of her friends
were still on the playground
enjoying the beauty of the day.
Suddenly, to my surprise,
she leaped in front of me, raised her arms
and pleaded, "Pick me up! Pick me up!
I want them to see you carry me!"

Sensing urgency,
I unhesitatingly complied,
though she's rather tall for that.
"Hi, Andy!" she called
to attract immediate attention,
and then I knew that
I was her "show and tell"
and I was glad.

KEEP ME AFRAID

"I want no man on board
who does not fear the whale."
Words of the captain in *Moby Dick*.

Only he who stands in awe can be trusted
with a great and difficult task.
Teaching is such a task—
yes, more, it is an art,
and no one does well
who thinks that he has mastered it.

The Christian teacher knows
that the gospel dwarfs both methods and men;
therefore the only fitting thing
for the preacher to do with his best sermon
or the teacher to do with his best "lesson"
is to ask God to forgive.
So great is the errand
that one needs forgiveness
before the effort,
and during and after it.

How relieved I would be if I could always
move with serene and unwavering confidence.
I don't like to "run scared" to class;
but deep within me I am sure that
once I cease to be afraid
I will no longer really be alive.
So, Lord, stay with me,
but keep me afraid.

SOGGY CEREAL AND TEPID TEA

When I remember that I am a parent,
and think of God as Father,
I recall a special breakfast
brought to me in bed.

We awoke early
to the sound of hurrying feet.
We wondered what they were up to,
our four- and eight-year-olds;
but soon it came—
breakfast in bed.

It was an elaborate menu:
chilled burnt toast, with peanut butter;
eggs, fried, and chilled, too;
soggy cereal,
(the milk had been added too soon)
and tepid tea!
A horrendous mix.

When they stepped out for a moment
to get something they'd forgotten (heaven forbid!)
my wife whispered,
"You're going to have to eat this, I can't!"
And I did.

I didn't eat as a gourmet,
for it wasn't gourmet cooking;
I didn't even eat as a hungry man
for I wasn't hungry.

I ate it as a father
because it was made for me;
I was expected to;
they had faith in me.
And I ate because it was served on eager feet
and with starry eyes.

I think of my poor service to God
as teacher, parent,
interpreter of the Good News.
I know that my offerings are soggy,
tepid, and unfit,
but my Father receives them
and even blesses them—
not because I am good
but because he is!

REAL LIVING

"All real living is meeting,"
said Martin Buber,
and meeting is an art.
It is losing and finding,
giving and receiving,
offering and surrendering.
In meeting, persons are changed
without frontal intent or strategy,
for meeting is enjoyment,
appreciation of personhood,
uniqueness and difference.

Deeper than any level of dialog
is enjoyment of another person.
We are not friends
until we have deliberately
"wasted" time together.
Then intertwining growth takes place,
and we are human together.

But such meeting cannot be measured.
It can only be experienced
and explored.

WHO READS JOHNNY?

I knew a tall man once
who endeared himself to children
because he took them seriously.
He respected them as persons
and proved it by reaching down to their level.
I mean this, literally;
he would stoop down, kneeling sometimes
to look into their eyes
and to really hear them.
He played with them,
but never as toys,
for he knew that no person is ever a toy.

In education, as in all human relationships,
the question is not so much,
why Johnny can't read
as, who reads Johnny?

Our Lord knew what was in men.
He read well and carefully
each person's mind and heart.
Love's library is people;
it reads the individual
and aims to see and understand
each person, one by one.
If we care, we will be alert
to mood and feeling.

We will know that our reading assignment,
as teachers or parents,
is that living, feeling,
learning person.

In more ways than one,
life's most important task
is to learn to read.

OLD CUPS

I stood in a famous museum
and viewed a collection of old cups,
some from centuries past.

Once these cups were fitted to lips and hands,
made for those who were to use them;
they weren't only to be looked at,
but were needed for what they could contain.

They must have been carefully fitted,
or were they?
Perhaps they never did fit the lip or the hand
and that's why they became museum pieces!

Our ways of speaking are like cups;
they are meant to carry meaning,
but they must be fitted
to those who hunger and thirst.

I face the painful question:
are my ways of saying things
blocking what I mean to say?
Am I in creative relationship
with those whom I would reach?
Or, are my honed and labored phrases
only museum pieces?

OPEN TO NEWNESS

The Mona Lisa was on exhibition
in a famous museum of art,
and we went to see.

I went to see and remember,
but I was robbed,
robbed of a memory.
At least, I can't recall
what was worth remembering.
I hardly saw the masterpiece.
At best, a brief glimpse,
because, you see,
we had to keep the lines moving.

"Keep the lines moving, keep the lines moving . . . "
Over and over, with rhythmic repetition,
the uniformed officers spoke their command;
and that's about all I remember.

I know it was necessary
to have order,
for there were many of us;
but the order defeated the purpose.
It was high price to pay.

I think how easy it is for the teacher
to police great meanings
right out the door.
How often, when newness and vision break in
and wait to be shared by some enchanted child

have we, the teachers, been preoccupied
with the orderly arrangement of class cards,
or with roll call, or rubbers,
or some other laudable trivia!

Father, protect me
from the antiseptic emptiness
of the artificial life.
Help me with my priorities
so that I may see,
see the difference between the sterile neatness
of death
and the untidy ferment of creation and life.

Keep me open to newness and surprise,
and help me never to crush anything
that is trying to be born
or crying for room.

THE BEAUTY OF BOLDNESS

Every adult
needs the experience
of playing on the floor
with a boisterous two-year-old.
It is a lesson in
being taken advantage of,
an education in the beauty of boldness.

Let him have his way,
that little one.
He'll not only
sit on your chest
and bounce on your stomach;
he'll pummel you,
rumple you, caress you
and nuzzle you.

He'll cry "More!"
He'll come as he pleases
and go as he pleases.
This is living in the freedom
of being loved.

"Let us therefore come boldly
Unto the throne of grace."

I THINK OF THE FIELDS

If only I could be done
with this extracurricular suffering
I've been experiencing lately,
I could get on with my teaching
or at least begin my preparation!

But then there's the absolution.
I heard it anew the other day.
I sat and drank it in.
New meanings leaped out at me;
new healings happened deep within.
I think of the fields in spring,
how tempered steel roughs up the matted soil.
I ponder the cruel kindness
of the harrow, the disc, and the plow,
and I know that without these
there would be only waste
of warm spring rains.

Can it be that suffering isn't extracurricular at all?
Is it, rather, a part of that core curriculum
of birth and life and death?
and Life?

STRONG WORDS

It happened at the market not long ago;
I know, for I was there.

A very young child,
enchanted by the goodies,
wandered too far.
Suddenly a cry!
The answer was quick in coming,
but already there were tears.
I heard the mother's words of comfort:
"You know I wouldn't leave you;
you're my boy!"

Great words, strong words
to set a child's world right again.

But where can *I* find words
in the eclipses and blackouts
of despair?
Are there words
big enough to match my human cry?

"Take heart, my son,
your sins are forgiven."
God's answer in the darkness,
big enough and strong enough
for me.

SILENCE-BREAKERS

"God is silence, but in Jesus Christ
he has broken that silence."
Ever since one of the greatest
of New Testament scholars said that
in my hearing,
I've thought of it and quoted it often.

God is unknowable at the depth
at which I must know him,
unless he makes himself known—
unknowable to me, the sinner,
unknowable as Savior,
as mercy,
until he reveals himself
in the person of Jesus Christ.

But God has shattered the silence,
has stepped into the void
and bridged the chasm.
And, since he has,
you and I are meant to be silence-breakers.
Life is mission,
and that mission is Christ,
our Lord.

THE ALWAYS PEOPLE

It really wasn't much,
just a brown paper bag
with a space stick,
a few salted peanuts "for now"
a handful of cookies "to take home"—
something to comfort a child
as she returned
from the doctor's office.
But when she saw it
she exclaimed,
"Oh, grandma *always* remembers!"

It was the way she strung out
the "al-ways"
that impressed me.
It reminded me that every life,
if it is to grow strong,
must have some "always people" in it,
persons who make up a supporting community,
the bearing parts
in the structure of a life.

Who are the "always people"
in your existence,
who have surely remembered you
and prayed for you today?

JOY IS A CHIPMUNK

Joy is a chipmunk;
it peeks out at you from behind things.
It darts and scurries, dances and frolics,
as long as you don't look for it too carefully
or approach it too swiftly.
Ambush it, and it will disappear
to reappear, but farther away.
Concentrate on it, and it is gone.
Ask yourself if you are happy,
and it is away!
But forget yourself in the moment's frolic
or the immediate task,
and it comes closer
to perch on your shoe,
climb up your leg,
and eat out of your hand.

FAITH GNAWS TOO

"Yes, doubt does keep gnawing
at one's faith."
I said it to a friend,
my friend in deep distress.
I said it to encourage,
but quickly he replied,
without a moment's hesitation,
"But faith keeps gnawing
at our doubts, too!"

It was a great response.
I am strengthened by it.
Intending to comfort,
I was comforted.
Today I walk more boldly
as I say:
Yes, doubt does gnaw at my faith,
but faith gnaws, too,
and faith has better teeth!

HE'S STILL AROUND

Since I'm a teacher,
no matter where I am,
I can never be more
than "the boy with the lunch."

I've often wondered about that boy.
Who was he,
and what really happened to him on that day?
Surely, he couldn't be the same again,
after seeing his lunch in those hands,
and the large crowd satisfied
from his little bag!

It couldn't have been much of a lunch
by the time Jesus got hold of it.
After all, fish get smaller by the minute
once they're caught and cooked;
and sandwiches are pretty crumby
when a boy has carried them
for half a day.

No, it wasn't much of a lunch
until Jesus blessed it!

But I hope the boy didn't make excuses
or hesitate.
Because if he did,
he showed that he'd forgotten
who was around.

A pretty crumby lesson plan,
some pretty fishy thoughts
I bring to class.
Only a miracle can save them,
but I mustn't apologize
or waste God's time explaining.
He's still around,
and miracles are his business.

MANY GATES

There are many gates
to the City of Man's Soul.
The teacher's joy and challenge
is in finding and unlocking them.

There are many methods
to match the subtly shifting situations
and infinitely various persons.
It has been wisely said
that "the worst method is the one
that's used all the time."
Any method becomes bad
when it is used unresponsively.

Teaching is response.
In Jesus we see the wise synthesis
of all teaching methods.
In his classroom without walls,
with the world as his visual aid,
he orchestrated them all:
the story, the parable,
the sermon,
the quick and probing question.

Many gates.
Love seeks, finds, and uses all.

YOU WILL MISS ME

"You will miss me when I die."
She was only five,
and said it
from behind a towering
piece of strawberry pie!

Grandma and granddaddy knew
that her mother was having a party
that evening,
a thing for grown-ups.
"Dinner will be late," we said,
"and not much for a little one,
so let's take her out."

We went to a special place
mostly to watch her
and listen to her enjoy.

It was a hearty meal for her:
eggs and toast and milk,
and then, to make it festive,
that piece of strawberry pie.
"You will miss me when I die,"
and quickly she added
for our consolation,
"but I think you will die
before I die."

What was she thinking?
What made her say it,
this little one,
what traffic flowed within her mind?
Could it be some thoughts like these?
"M-m-m, good!
So red, so juicy sweet,
and so much white on top.
They love me, they really do.
They call me 'mine.'
I'm theirs, but it's kind of sad-glad
because I will die and they will miss me."

Whatever she thought
she must have sensed belonging;
she must have felt some cherishing
and enjoying.
This is enough,
the greatest and the best.

DELIVER US!

From classrooms
that creak and squeak,
rule-ridden and constrictive,
defensive and rigid,
reflecting the neuroses
of adults
rather than the needs
of children;
from prison-houses
of artificiality and anxiety,
where nothing breathes,
Good Lord,
deliver us!

A SACRAMENT OF SILENCE

There will be some silence in any class.
Sometimes it may be just dead silence
with nothing happening.
This is a terrifying thing;
one can only ask the spirit to brood over it,
creating again,
repeating the first miracle,
turning nothing into something.

But there are other silences,
the silence of reflection,
of confession, or reaffirmation,
or, the silence of recognition,
affection, opposition,
or even the silence of struggle
and decision.

After years of teaching I'm not as afraid of silence
as I once was; it helps to say to oneself:
"Don't forget, God can make a sacrament
of silence."

SHE WAS RIGHT

I won't forget a small child
who wouldn't say "thank you."
It happened in the doctor's office.
Only a routine check,
but this was followed by a shot,
and the little one had cried.
Now the tears were dried
and it was time to go.

Without thinking, I said,
"Tell the doctor, 'thank you.' "
Bless her, she wouldn't say it;
and, of course, she was right.
She wouldn't say what she didn't feel;
she wouldn't be false
to please a parent.
Such is the integrity of the child.

I think how we rear our altars
of adult pride,
encouraging hypocrisy and hollow courtesy
by unwise and thoughtless commands.
How we need to subject each request
to the rigid test of a child's integrity,
remembering that a wise man once said:
"Nearly all the truth that is told in this world
is told by children."

NEXT EXIT: AMEN

The Apostles' Creed
is like a freeway.
Once you're on it
you have to respect the signs.
When you say,
"I believe in God"
thought leads to thought
as each phrase unfolds
its depth of meaning,
sweeping you along.

Then, as you look ahead,
you see it:
"Next exit: Amen!"

The Holy Trinity,
three persons, one God—
suggests impossible arithmetic.
But don't worry.

It really tells us that
the God of the Bible
is a very great God,
and though the mind cannot comprehend him
the heart can receive him.

There's a wholeness
that mustn't be violated.
So, once you've said "God,"
there's no place to get off
Until you reach the exit:
"Amen."

74

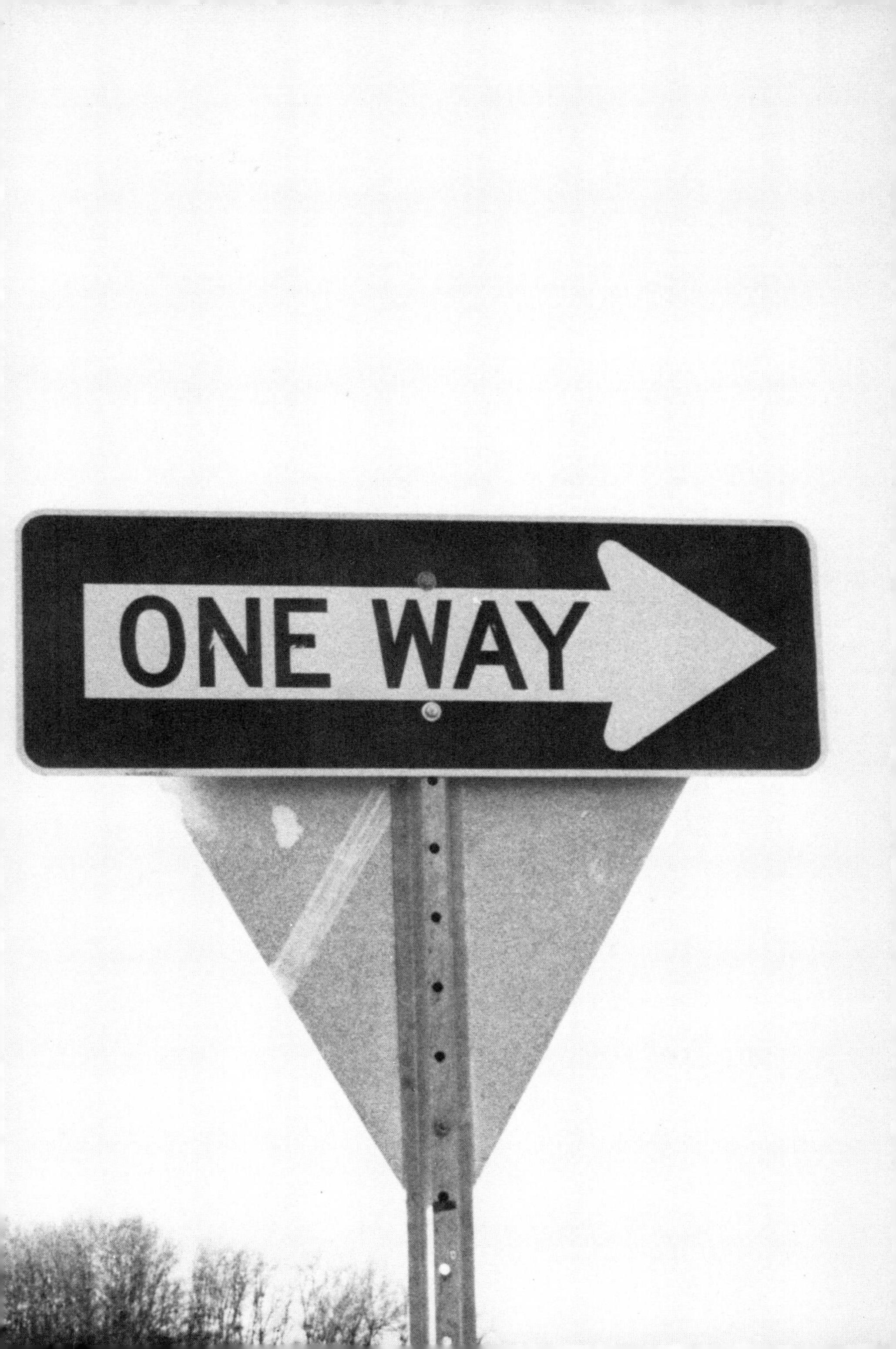
ONE WAY

A RIFT IN THE SKY

There are "Stephen moments"
in history,
moments when there is
a breakthrough of goodness,
a rift in the sky.

Where God's Spirit is the teacher
there is vision,
at the cost of one's old life.
To really see Jesus
is to come and die,
to lose oneself,
moment by moment,
in caring participation
in the anguish of the ages.
It is to take sides
and make the stones fly!

They stoned Stephen,
and proud Saul became "the little one."
It was a trigger-event,
an end and a beginning,
the kind that provides
a hinge for history.

WHAT IS REVERENCE?

What is it,
this that we call reverence?

Is it masks and make-up?
Is it dotted Is and crossed Ts?
Is it a stately processions
of Thees and Thous,
goose-stepping in the corridors of one's mind?

Or,
is it the capacity to feel agony and ecstasy
and place all in the lap of God?
Is it honesty, awe, wonder,
gaiety and gladness,
each related to the Spirit in one's heart?

Or,
Is it, perhaps, just being yourself
in Christ's presence?

HE CAME TO ME

He came for a large gift,
but he came to me.
Yes, a large gift, but I had it to give,
for he asked for that
which all men have to give,
the gift of attention.
And he came to me!
He wanted "a little hunk of life,"
my life.

I gave him only half a gift,
for I was only partly present to him.
My thoughts wandered, my attention wavered;
I made other plans, I looked past him,
I ran ahead and away from him,
I wanted him to leave!

I wonder if he knew how I robbed him that day,
cheated him, betrayed him in his trust.
I wonder, is he hungry still?
I can only say, Good Lord, forgive.
Forgive, and grant me a "next time."

OUR FATHER

I prayed today,
prayed "Our Father."
An airport was my cathedral,
the busy one at Newark,
the crowded one in New Jersey.

I didn't fold my hands;
I didn't close my eyes,
or bow my head.
I looked straight at them,
I looked at God through them—
through my brothers and sisters.

I looked at "our Father"
through his hurrying,
hoping, trying, crying
family.

He looked right back at me
and smiled.

TAKE ALL THE RISKS

When I reflect on teaching,
I can't forget the words
of an Olympic ski champion,
a man for whom two minutes is a career:
"Go faster than you think you can
on every part of the course;
take all the risks."

Take all the risks.
Great words for one who is to teach.
Take the risk of loving;
it means that you'll be hurt.
Take the risk of listening;
it means that you will learn
and will have to change.
Take the risk of responding;
little by little, it will cost you
your life!

Teaching is response.
Learning occurs within relationships,
and relationship involves risk,
the risk of knowing and of being known.

THEY TOOK UP STONES

"And they took up stones
to stone him."
That's the way it was
when Jesus taught.

His parables were truth-traps,
baited to lure the listener
into the situation
before he could say, "Who, me?"

To teach is to confront, interpret, and reflect.
It is to leave the person
respectfully alone
with troublesome meanings,
and then to wait
while he wrestles and decides.
It is even to honor
the search for escape
and the right to say "No!"

But confrontation draws fire.
Wherever there's learning
there's change.
And change is pain,
the pain that sometimes angers
before it heals.

"They took up stones."

AFTER ALL

She was chattering to herself
in the back seat of the car,
talking and taking delight,
as four-year-olds do,
in herself
and the free frolic of her mind.

I listened,
as grown-ups do,
delighted, too,
as she talked much bigger
than she was.

Then, suddenly,
she spoke a sentence,
saying, "After all,"
and more suddenly still
she arrested me,
handcuffed and captured me,
with the sharp question:
"What does *after all* mean?"

A little child shall lead them
into humility.

OUR ALIVE ONE

Our little one,
our eager one,
our alive one—
I watched her with a candle,
a very special candle,
a Christmas candle,
a scented, many-colored candle.

She looked, she touched,
she held, she smelled;
and there I would have stopped,
but not the little one,
the alive one!

Suddenly, impulsively, she opened her mouth
and caressed the wax with her tongue,
straining to meet it,
to possess it,
to experience
with all her senses.

To learn is to live,
to be,
to grow
in the light of new knowledge.

Why do we fragment,
dissect,
destroy
the learner
in the learning?

Why will we deny our senses
and starve our feelings
in dreary alienation
and sensory death?

ALL THE LITTLE BOXES

The only time people are alike
is after they're dead.
Then rows of identical boxes can contain them.

The pity is that sometimes,
out of fear or indifference,
we teach in such a way as to force
living people into identical little boxes.
We give them no living room;
we make them into timid people
with trivial questions, looking for
pat and easy answers, and no courage
to ask the big ones.

Standardization, regimentation, homogenization—
these are smiling enemies within the gates.
Their friendly faces promise much,
belying their power to maim or crush the human spirit.
These are the servants of dullness
and henchmen of boredom.
Their aim is a stereotype
of docile people whose faces
blend into any crowd.

God help us to scuttle all the little boxes,
and to see that the ultimate heresy
is to want things neat!

THE MAD ONES

When Jesus chose an image
to speak of the Word
he didn't take a pebble
or even a pearl.
He chose a living seed;
and in his choice
was promise,
the promise that
the God who gives the seasons
does not desert his Word.

But seed time
is mad time.
Once every year
the farmer must succumb—
no, not succumb, achieve—
achieve a springtime madness,
the madness of throwing
his best away,
his very best seed.

Without this seedtime madness
there is no harvest gladness.

And so we teach,
we, the mad ones, the glad ones.

The seasons march slowly,
so slowly,
we die between the "left-rights."

We wait and work;
and work and wait.
Only the eyes of faith,
only the ears of faith
see clearly—or is it dimly?—
hear clearly—or is it faintly?—
the harvest with its song.

But as surely as God is faithful,
the fields will whiten
and our little acts will join
his mighty "Yes" in Christ, the Word.

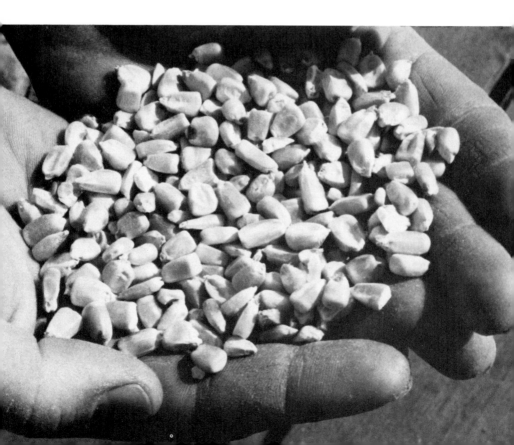

THAT WHITE DOG

How well I remember a year in junior high,
the year that was spoiled by a white dog.
My brother and I rode our horses every day,
ten miles on country roads.
This was no hardship, for we loved our horses;
the problem was that half-way to town
there lived that nice farmer with his nasty dog.

This dog had a special talent for terrifying horses.
He would lie waiting in the tall grass,
leap at their noses from the edge of the road,
then run in front of them, nipping as he ran.
Several times we were almost thrown,
and once, at least, when it was raining
one of us landed in a mud puddle
and we had to return home.

Weeks and months were spoiled by that dog.
In the mornings and afternoons
I remember my mind wandering during the lessons,
and my saying to myself, "How, oh how, are we going
to deal with that dog?" And at night,
I would pray, "Now I lay me down to sleep,"
and think, "but what about the dog?"
"I pray Thee, Lord, my soul to keep.
Oh, yes, but there's that dog!"

I smile now as I speak of that dog.
He was a child's problem in a child's world,
and I am no longer a child;
but today I have other white dogs.

Everyone, from the littlest to the greatest,
from the youngest to the oldest,
has a white dog.
One of the tasks of the teacher
is to locate the learner as a person,
find him where he lives, white dog and all.
All of us are troubled people.
If I think of someone as having no burden,
I only prove that I do not know that person.

PERPETUAL SURPRISE

I'll not forget that hot August day
when I stopped for a coke
and got "pentecost."

I, a very young pastor,
two months in my parish,
hot and thirsty
from walking from house to house,
felt it.
I sensed in my very soul
what I'd never experienced so deeply before
and seldom so dramatically since:
the Almighty Father
really cares for me
and all his people;
he's "got the whole world
in his hands!"

Can it be that grace takes us by surprise
in the midst of the ordinary and the repeated?
Why shouldn't this be so,
since grace is from outside us,
not within?
It is God's interruption,
his wonderful invasion.

Grace is God at his unpredictable best.
No vision of Christ duplicates another,
for love defies the stereotype.
To believe is to live in perpetual surprise
and expectation.

94

TAKK FOR ALT

She was not quite ninety-seven
when she died.
One who waited at her side
heard her say it:
"Takk for alt" "Thank you for everything."
It was her home-going word to God.

Like a good guest
she addressed her Host.
She spoke as one well-taught,
well-taught by life,
by memory and expectation!

To be gift-conscious is to be wise;
to know whom to thank is grace indeed.
To know the gift and love the Giver,
to have learned life's dearest lesson,
is to be rich toward God.